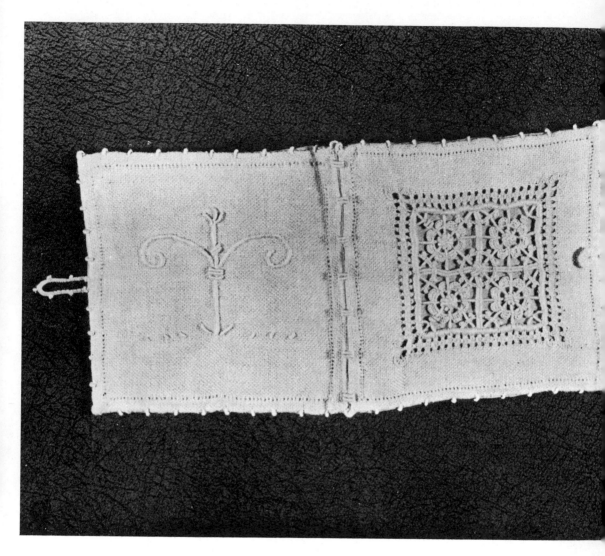

FRONTISPIECE   A TRADITIONAL NEEDLE-BOOK, BY AUTHOR

CUT-WORK EMBROIDERY
and How to Do It

Oenone Cave

Dover Publications, Inc.
NEW YORK

Published in Canada by General Publishing Company, Ltd., 30 Lesmill Road,
Don Mills, Toronto, Ontario.
Published in the United Kingdom by Constable and Company, Ltd., 10 Orange
Street, London WC2H 7EG.

This Dover edition, first published in 1982, is an altered republication of the work
first published in 1963 by Vista Books, London, under the title *Linen Cut-Work*.

Manufactured in the United States of America
Dover Publications, Inc.
180 Varick Street
New York, N.Y. 10014

Library of Congress Cataloging in Publication Data

Cave, Oenone.
   Cut-work embroidery and how to do it.

   Rev. ed. of: Linen cut-work. London: Vista Books, 1963.
(Vista embroidery handbooks)
   Bibliography: p.
   Includes index.
   1. Drawn-work. 2. Punched work. 3 Lace and lace making.
I. Title. II. Series: Vista embroidery handbooks.
TT785.C38 1982   746.44   81-17307
ISBN 0-486-24267-6   AACR2

Contents

3

List of Illustrations

Metric Conversion Chart

CONVERTING INCHES TO CENTIMETERS AND YARDS TO METERS

mm — millimeters   cm — centimeters   m — meters

INCHES INTO MILLIMETERS AND CENTIMETERS
(Slightly rounded off for convenience)

inches	mm			inches	cm	inches	cm	inches	cm
⅛	3mm			5	12.5	21	53.5	38	96.5
¼	6mm			5½	14	22	56	39	99
⅜	10mm	or	1cm	6	15	23	58.5	40	101.5
½	13mm	or	1.3cm	7	18	24	61	41	104
⅝	15mm	or	1.5cm	8	20.5	25	63.5	42	106.5
¾	20mm	or	2cm	9	23	26	66	43	109
⅞	22mm	or	2.2cm	10	25.5	27	68.5	44	112
1	25mm	or	2.5cm	11	28	28	71	45	114.5
1¼	32mm	or	3.2cm	12	30.5	29	73.5	46	117
1½	38mm	or	3.8cm	13	33	30	76	47	119.5
1¾	45mm	or	4.5cm	14	35.5	31	79	48	122
2	50mm	or	5cm	15	38	32	81.5	49	124.5
2½	65mm	or	6.5cm	16	40.5	33	84	50	127
3	75mm	or	7.5cm	17	43	34	86.5		
3½	90mm	or	9cm	18	46	35	89		
4	100mm	or	10cm	19	48.5	36	91.5		
4½	115mm	or	11.5cm	20	51	37	94		

YARDS TO METERS
(Slightly rounded off for convenience)

yards	meters	yards	meters	yards	meters	yards	meters	yards	meters
⅛	0.15	2⅛	1.95	4⅛	3.80	6⅛	5.60	8⅛	7.45
¼	0.25	2¼	2.10	4¼	3.90	6¼	5.75	8¼	7.55
⅜	0.35	2⅜	2.20	4⅜	4.00	6⅜	5.85	8⅜	7.70
½	0.50	2½	2.30	4½	4.15	6½	5.95	8½	7.80
⅝	0.60	2⅝	2.40	4⅝	4.25	6⅝	6.10	8⅝	7.90
¾	0.70	2¾	2.55	4¾	4.35	6¾	6.20	8¾	8.00
⅞	0.80	2⅞	2.65	4⅞	4.50	6⅞	6.30	8⅞	8.15
1	0.95	3	2.75	5	4.60	7	6.40	9	8.25
1⅛	1.05	3⅛	2.90	5⅛	4.70	7⅛	6.55	9⅛	8.35
1¼	1.15	3¼	3.00	5¼	4.80	7¼	6.65	9¼	8.50
1⅜	1.30	3⅜	3.10	5⅜	4.95	7⅜	6.75	9⅜	8.60
1½	1.40	3½	3.20	5½	5.05	7½	6.90	9½	8.70
1⅝	1.50	3⅝	3.35	5⅝	5.15	7⅝	7.00	9⅝	8.80
1¾	1.60	3¾	3.45	5¾	5.30	7¾	7.10	9¾	8.95
1⅞	1.75	3⅞	3.55	5⅞	5.40	7⅞	7.20	9⅞	9.05
2	1.85	4	3.70	6	5.50	8	7.35	10	9.15

AVAILABLE FABRIC WIDTHS

25"	65cm	50"	127cm
27"	70cm	54"/56"	140cm
35"/36"	90cm	58"/60"	150cm
39"	100cm	68"/70"	175cm
44"/45"	115cm	72"	180cm
48"	122cm		

AVAILABLE ZIPPER LENGTHS

4"	10cm	10"	25cm	22"	55cm
5"	12cm	12"	30cm	24"	60cm
6"	15cm	14"	35cm	26"	65cm
7"	18cm	16"	40cm	28"	70cm
8"	20cm	18"	45cm	30"	75cm
9"	22cm	20"	50cm		

Bibliography

Giving the following titles of 'Lace' books as a bibliography for Linen Cut-Work may seem misleading; but there seems to be no publication wholly devoted to this type of embroidery. Cut-work is either treated as a forerunner, together with drawn-work, of needle-point lace, or as a basis of many open-work embroideries with specific names; so it is under such headings that most references to Cut-work are to be found.

A MANUAL OF LACE   J. W. Pethebridge

THE ROMANCE OF LACE   Mary E. Jones

A HISTORY OF HAND-MADE LACE   Mrs F. N. Jackson

POUR CONNAITRE LA DENTELLE   Paulis

LACE AND LACE-MAKING   Marian Powys

THE LACE BOOK   J. F. Caplin

ANTICHE TRINE ITALIANE, Vols I and II   Elisa Ricci

LEGEND AND HISTORY OF LACE   Mrs C. Popp

PATTERNS   Mathio Pagani (*Box in the Victoria and Albert Museum Library*)

PATTERNS   G. Franco (*Box in the Victoria and Albert Museum Library*)

ORNAMENTS   G. A. Vavassole

Foreword

I HAVE written this book in the hope of preserving the history of an ancient craft. I trust it may also encourage the embroiderer of today to accept a challenge in yet another field of linen embroidery.

I acknowledge with gratitude my happy associations with fellow workers, and the kind assistance from my many friends in the Lake District, without whom I would never have learnt the craft in the beginning – nor would I have been able to piece together the fascinating story of the nineteenth-century revival of this traditional embroidery.

In particular, I should like to mention Mrs Parsons, Curator of the Ruskin Museum at Coniston; Mrs Tucker, the owner of the last surviving lace-making industry at Grasmere; and Mr Harold Dawson of Coniston, who, with his wife, was one of the original Lakeland craftsmen. Mr Dawson, Mrs Betty Hodgson of Grange-over-Sands, and Mrs Constantinesco of Torver kindly lent me their beautiful samples of 'Greek Lace' to be photographed for inclusion in this book.

The Embroiderers' Guild have given much encouragement to the continuance of 'Greek Lace' (Ruskin Linen Work), and to widen the field of its practice. I also acknowledge the kind help of the authorities of the Victoria and Albert Museum, mentioning particularly Miss Wardle of the Textile Department, the Photographic Section and the facilities enjoyed in the Library. The Italian Institute of Culture, in London, was most helpful in gaining me permission to reproduce pictures of original 'Linen Cut-work'.

It was most encouraging to learn from Constance Howard, A.R.C.A., of the modern approach to linen cut-work as practised by her students at the Goldsmiths' School. The two plates included in this book amply illustrate the effectiveness of modern design carried out in traditional stitchery.

Publisher's Note

This book was originally written and published in England; therefore some of the threads and fabrics listed in the Introduction and throughout the book may not be available. Other threads and fabrics of similar weight which will produce the same results may be substituted—check with your local needlework shop or department. When buying thread and fabric, be sure to purchase a sufficient amount to complete the project; it is often impossible to match shades later because dye lots vary.

Introduction

SINCE man first interwove strands of natural fibres to form the warp and weft of textile, the elaboration and decoration of such fabrics has been the answer to every embroiderer's ambition to express beauty in what she creates.

Linen, one of the oldest materials, includes all the yarns and fabrics spun or woven from flax fibres. This smooth and lustrous cloth has been used as the basis for embroidery since the earliest periods of human history, and the gossamer delicacy yet strength of the thread fits it for the finest embroidery and lace-making. It is admirably suited to all types of counted thread embroidery because, for this, the evenness of the warp and weft plays an essential part in the success of the finished work. This is especially true in Linen Cut-work.

Whether a fine linen or a more substantial quality is chosen, the even texture of hand-woven material is of the greatest value. The speed of production by machine has outmoded the hand loom, but it is still possible to obtain hand-woven linen. Otherwise, Glenshee Evenweave is the best substitute; it is made in three shades, ivory, cream and natural, and is available in 22-inch and 52-inch widths.

The weight of the linen thread must vary according to the thickness of the background material. Knox's pure linen needlework thread (a 'Linen Lace Thread') can be bought in skeins and is spun in the following shades: white, natural, whitish brown (off-white or warm ivory), grey (off-white, not grey), Paris (slightly greenish fawn), Ecru (yellowish off-white) and cream (paler yellowish off-white). The size of the thread ranges from 25, 30, 35, 40, 45, 60, to the very finest size, 70.

The shade of the material and thread may match or contrast. A dark thread worked on a pale or natural linen, or vice versa, looks very effective. For linen cut-work used as a decoration on table linen, a matching thread and material is perhaps most in keeping with the simplicity of the traditional designs. It is customary to use a rather coarser thread when working the open hem than the thread chosen for the lace-like fillings.

Colour, by tradition, is not introduced in either the thread or the material, although a background of coloured silk is sometimes attached behind the open-work, in articles such as a cushion cover, or a needle case. This will enhance the lacy filling; a polished table has the same effect, showing off table linen to perfection.

One of the attractions of linen cut-work is the comparatively small number of materials which are required, none of which are either expensive or different from those usually found in a well-equipped work-box. The most important asset is a pair of small, finely-pointed scissors; a clear tape-measure is essential, also a few strong steel pins and a reel of tacking cotton.

Needles vary according to the weight of thread used; a medium to fine tapestry needle is used for working the open hem, while the sharps are best for stitching the lace-like filling.

A backing cloth is temporarily attached to the linen to stretch the fabric evenly and provide a firm foundation upon which to work. Originally of parchment, any medium-weight vinyl or synthetic leather-cloth backing may be used; the needle-book in the Frontispiece was photographed on a background of leather-cloth.

CHAPTER I

The History of an Ancient Craft

CUT-WORK is the name given by the ancient writers to denote specific types of needlework to which the drawing out of threads is a preliminary. It embraces various forms of open-work, and is derived from the primitive art of netting. The history of the craft supports its claim to the unique position as the link between embroidery and lace-making.

Embroidery is fundamentally different from lace-making in that the one ornaments existing material, while the other produces a fabric which is itself ornamental. The open-work designs of linen cut-work are built up into independent fabric, but whether the open-work structure is well inside the linen background or worked as an edging, the cut-work 'lace' never becomes entirely free of the adherent material.

Lace-making and embroidery are often worked in conjunction, to adorn the home and to enrich the dress of every class of society; this is especially true of cut-work, in which embroidered motifs are interspersed with the lace fillings.

The word *lace* is a derivation of the Latin *lacinia*, meaning 'fringe'. It is interesting to note that in the twelfth century, at the opening of the tomb of St Cuthbert in Durham Cathedral, a monk named Reginald described the Saint's shroud as having 'a fringe of linen threads an inch long, surmounted by a border worked upon the threads'; this suggests that open-work was practised sometime before the same stitches and methods came to be recognised as the first needle-made laces.

Between the thirteenth and sixteenth centuries the earliest forms of lace-making, better described as cut-work, were known in France as *point coupé*, in Italy as *punto tagliato* and in Germany as *opus seissum*. During this period of history the craft was confined principally to the nunneries, being used to adorn priests' sacramental robes and for other ecclesiastical purposes. The stamped open-worked decoration used inside coffins, known as *pinking*, owes its origin to the trimmings of open-work on grave clothes.

After the fifteenth century the charm of cut-work and early lace-making flourished in convents, at Court and in the homes of the nobility. It became the occupation of ladies of high society to ornament their fine linen with trimmings of cut-work and lace. The making and wearing of lace also became part of the life of the peasants; but, as is always the case when an art is adopted by the lower classes, it was turned to more practical uses, and the peasant shirt and hood were favourite articles for ornamentation.

The Ionian Isles, in particular Corfu and Zante, were celebrated for a cut-work known as Greek Lace, otherwise referred to as Roman Lace or Gothic Point (PLATE 1), which took precedence among laces between 1480 and 1620 (PLATE 2). Exactly where from, and when, Greek lace found its way to the shores of Italy remains uncertain, but Greece is known to have been the source of much fine needlework, and history recalls the great influence the Greeks had on their neighbours, especially Venice, the home of so many laces.

During the sixteenth century the original character of the thick stitching of cut-work changed (PLATE 3); the geometrical outlines were augmented by fillings made with the same style of patterns, but which included more ambitious forms, such as half-circles, triangles and wheels. Gradually Greek lace was merged into the better-known Italian *reticella* (PLATE 4), which is recognised as the first needle-point lace, forerunner of the veritable laces. The craft then acquired an individual character of its own (PLATE 5).

Lace-making since its earliest days has always been divided into two categories: needle-point lace and bobbin lace. Charles Blanc wrote of the distinction between the two: 'The dominant character of pillow lace is the soft blending of its forms, the needle is to the bobbin what the pencil is to the stump. The pattern . . . of which the definition becomes softened when wrought in pillow lace . . . is depicted with crispness by the needle.'

The seventeenth century was the heyday of lace production. Some of the laces were called after the stitches (*punti*) employed: Point de Neige, Gros point de Venise, Carolina point, Rose point lace, and Hollie point (a corruption of 'Holy point', used to denote church laces in which the pattern depicted scriptural subjects or contained sacred emblems). Other laces were named after the locality of their manufacture; this tends to be misleading, because often the adopted home of the lace is far from its place of origin.

Though Venice continued to enjoy supremacy in the art of lace-making, the Italian fashion of both men and women wearing lace spread throughout Europe. It found special favour in the court of Elizabeth I of England, where the ruffs were often made up of scallops of cut-work (PLATE 6). Other interesting articles, such as coverlets, cushions, handkerchiefs, cuffs and veils, have been preserved and are now on display in the Victoria and Albert Museum (PLATE 7).

Queen Catherine of Medici, the Italian queen of Henry II of France, laid the foundation of the French lace industry; she patronised the Italian designer Federico Vinciolo, because his patterns were so very suitable for the gadrooned collars and high wired revers of lace, both so popular at that period (PLATE 8). Vinciolo, in turn, dedicated his series of patterns, dated 1587, to the Queen of France, Louise de Lorraine, wife of Henry III.

Cyprus lace, an early form of cut-work almost identical with Greek lace, is of very ancient origin, and the beautiful samples of the thirteenth and fourteenth centuries often carried out in silver and gold threads, must not be confused with the peasant embroidery of a later date, which was worked mainly for commercial gain.

A few of the varying types of cut-work are the Danish Hedebo white embroidery, the Mexican open-work, the Czechoslovakian cut-work, the Russian torchon lace of the Ukraine, and the drawn- and cut-work from Spain and Sicily. Some are wrought in heavy threads of bold design, and others, especially the chalice veils, are of such delicate material that it is a marvel they have survived.

After the sumptuary laws enforced the abandoning of colour and rich elaboration in embroidery, the embroideresses in convent and castle alike turned their attention to white work, drawn-work and cut-work, perfecting the craft in every detail. Venetian workers, already pastmasters at producing embroideries inspired by delicate patterns such as are found on the borders of missals and arabesques of Near Eastern origin, soon wanted to go beyond the limits of the Greek lace designs which were governed by the threads of the material. The cut-out areas were enlarged more and more, until an edging called *punto-in-aria* gave the lace-maker complete freedom of design (PLATE 9); a padded roll remained the only connection between the edging and the fabric.

Paintings and manuscripts portray cut-work earlier than any existing specimens of the work. One of the earliest portraits, which can be seen in the Accademia in Venice, was painted by Carpaccio in about 1520; in this painting the cuff of the lady's dress includes a cut-work design found in Vecellio's *Corona della nobili e virtuose donne*, a pattern book published eighty years later in 1600. Other artists, such as Allori and Bassoni, loved to depict embroidery in their paintings.

Samplers, or sam-cloths, became treasured specimens of inspiration, handed down from one generation to another, being a more economical but a far more laborious way of tuition than pattern books (PLATES 10 and 11). Pattern books by Antonio Taghiante (1528) and Nicolo d'Aristotile (1530) described in detail the methods and stitches of cut-work and needle-made lace, which are identical with those used in the execution of Greek lace. Further books of patterns were Parasole's *Pietiosa Gemma delle donne* (1600), Federico Vinciolo's *I singolare nuovi disegni per lavori di biancheria* (1587), and Giacomo Franco's *Nuova Inventione* (1596). These are a few of the manuscripts treasured by the library of the Victoria and Albert Museum, and they give the student every opportunity to acquaint herself with traditional designs.

Thus the evolution of cut-work may be followed; the story shows interesting connections with the Middle Ages by way of drawn-work, and an association with the birth of true lace-making in the sixteenth century through needle-point; and it tells of the revival of the craft in the English Lake District during the nineteenth century (PLATE 12).

Lace has long been a treasure of the private collector, and has always been preserved as an heirloom; it has a pride of place among the rich embellishments of costume and furnishings which are enjoyed by royalty and peasant alike. There have been periods in history when fortunes were squandered on the purchase of lace, while at other times its popularity has waned to no account, but, to quote a saying of an old Swedish lace worker, 'Lace craft slumbers, it does not die'.

PLATE 2   FRAGMENT OF NEEDLE-POINT LACE FROM ZANTE,
IONIAN ISLES (*from the collection of lace, Needlework
Development Scheme*)

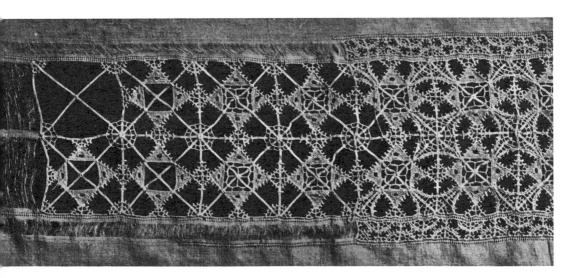

PLATE 3   SIXTEENTH-CENTURY UNFINISHED CUT-WORK
ON DRAWN LINEN (*Palermo Museum*)

PLATE 4 SIXTEENTH-CENTURY ITALIAN SAMPLER OF CUT-
WORK (*Greek Lace*): FILLINGS, MOTIFS AND
NEEDLE-POINT EDGING

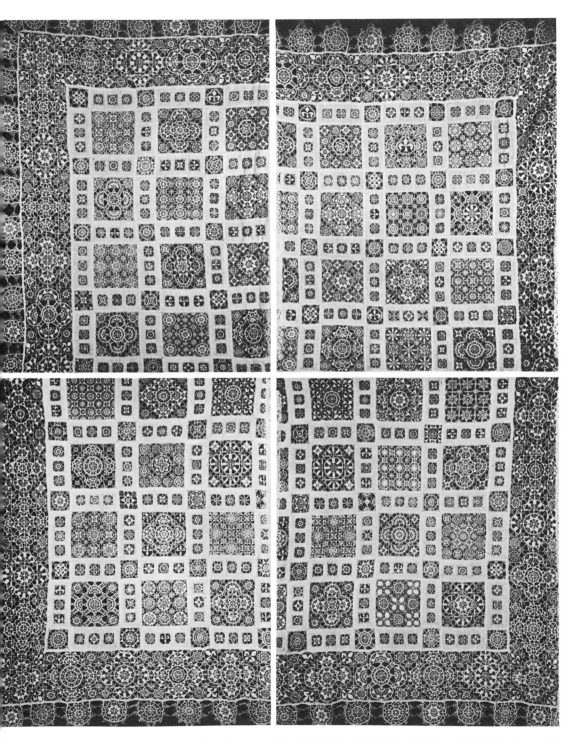

PLATE 5   TABLECLOTH IN FOUR PARTS: RETICELLA AND
PUNTO-IN-ARIA (*Cooper Union Museum, New York*)

PLATE 6   PORTRAIT OF 'A LADY', THOUGHT TO BE THE
COUNTESS OF ESSEX (*belonging to His Grace the Duke
of Portland*)

PLATE 7   HANDKERCHIEF: SIXTEENTH-CENTURY RETI-
CELLA LACE, EDGING OF PUNTO-IN-ARIA (*Victoria
and Albert Museum*)

CLAVDIA HENRICI II REGIS GALLA... FILIA CAROLI
LOTHARINGIAE DVCIS CONIVX

PLATE 8 PORTRAIT OF THE DUCHESS CLAUDE OF
LORRAINE BY CLOUET, 1555 (*Munich Gallery*)

PLATE 9   AN EDGING OF PUNTO-IN-ARIA (*belonging to Mrs Constantinesco, Torver, Coniston*)

PLATE 10 SAMPLER OF DRAWN- AND CUT-WORK,
ENGLISH (*Crown copyright, Victoria and Albert Museum*)

24

PLATE II   SAMPLER OF DRAWN- AND CUT-WORK FROM
GERMANY (*Crown copyright, Victoria and Albert
Museum*)

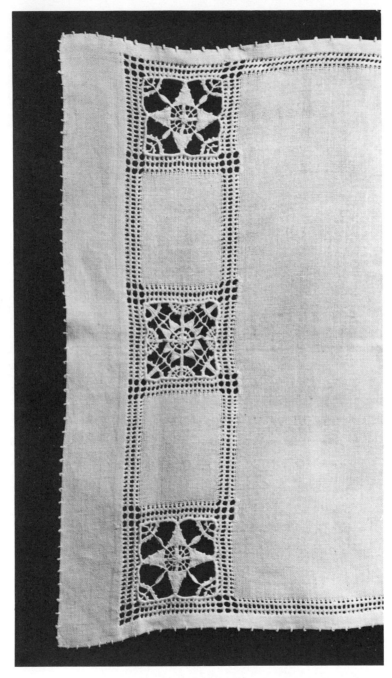

PLATE 12 CHAIR BACK WORKED BY THE LATE MRS
HAROLD DAWSON, ONE OF THE ORIGINAL
LAKELAND WORKERS

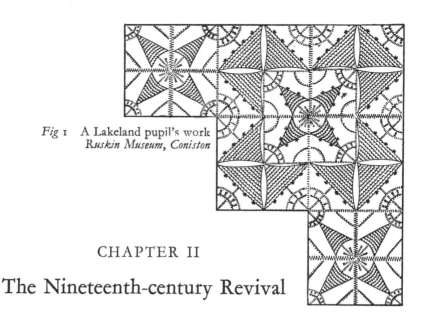

CHAPTER II

The Nineteenth-century Revival

D URING the nineteenth century another variation of cut-work appeared, which was known by the traditional name of Greek Lace.

John Ruskin, born in 1819 in the English Lake District, had very close ties with Italy, especially Venice. These, with his love of the arts, may well have led him to realise how suitable the original Greek lace patterns would look on the sun-bleached handspun linen then being produced by the country folk round his beloved Lakeland home Brantwood, on the shores of Lake Coniston.

Exactly how the lace patterns were brought to the Lake District is not known, but it seems obvious that Ruskin was instrumental in their introduction. Ruskin believed that young and old should 'be busily occupied in one of the natural pursuits of life, either in the field or in the home'. The abundance of flax growing in the fertile Langdale Valley and the weaving of linen, which was now being embroidered by the new method, seemed to him to provide a situation where his wish might come true. Ably helped and encouraged by a near neighbour, Albert Flemming, who came to live at 'The Crag', Elterwater, Ruskin strove to improve the poverty of the local inhabitants.

The Reverend Canon Rawnsley, a keen follower and friend of Ruskin, tells us in his book *Ruskin and the English Lakes* 'the re-introduction of the spinning-wheel into the cottage homes of Cumberland and Westmorland is a fairy tale that for Ruskin's sake should be told'.

Since 1819 the spinning-wheel had lain idle, because of the advent of machines; Wordsworth laments the changed 'silence' of the pastoral dales in the first lines of his sonnet *The Spinning-Wheel*:

'Grief thou hast lost an ever ready friend
Now that the cottage spinning-wheel is mute.'

Some sixty years later, an old spinning-wheel which stood as an ornament in Mr Flemming's drawing-room caused the founding of the Langdale Linen Industry: an old lady visiting Mr Flemming could not resist the wheel. To her joy she found that even at the age of 87 her fingers were still deft enough to spin on the old wheel. Encouraged by her host's enthusiasm the old lady opened her home, St Martin's Cottage, to those who would come and learn to spin and weave.

Through the ingenuity of the local carpenter and the bobbin turner twelve new spinning-wheels were reassembled from the relics abandoned to attic and barn years before. The skill of spinning and weaving was still in the blood of the village people, and many of them could remember their parents and grandparents weaving harden-sark from the wool of the mountain sheep, often with only the glow from the fire for light.

The flax was handed out to the cottagers to wash and dry in the sun, and the tubs used for this process can still be seen standing outside some Lakeland homes. Once more the hum of the treadle and the click-click of the loom could be heard from these quaint spinning-galleries (PLATE 13) which, in days gone by, had been a feature of the local countryside. How pleased Wordsworth would have been to hear that familiar sound, to know his lament had not fallen on deaf ears.

'The work in all its aspects' – to use Ruskin's words – pleased him greatly; it also added a new impetus to village life. There were spinster tea parties and spinning 'dos', and the days preceding these occasions were taken up with baking so that nothing should interfere with the weaving and the spinning. No gossiping was tolerated, and we are told that passages from the poets or Ruskin's works were read aloud.

At first the hand-spun thread was coarse and uneven, but soon a perfect even-weave linen was in full production. Greek lace patterns were used (PLATE 14) and the craft thrived. Just how much the cottagers loved the enterprise may be summed up by the saying of a Langdale spinster to Mr Flemming: 'You may take my life, but you must not take my wheel!' Ruskin Work, as it is sometimes called, embroidered on Ruskin linen became yet another craft cherished to this day by the Lakeland people.

Miss Twelves, a pioneer worker and teacher, for thirty-five years successfully organised the Linen Industry, first in Westmorland and then from her cottage home Crosthwaite, near Keswick in Cumberland. Several beautiful samples of Greek lace (or Ruskin linen work) are now on display in the Ruskin Museum at Coniston; some of these may have been worked by Miss Twelves herself, while others are reputed to be the work of her pupils (*fig* 1).

The craft received the patronage of prominent people, including royalty, as well as the support gained by the visitors from many lands. In 1884 Ruskin gave his consent for his name to be used in connection with the craft, so that the *Ruskin Linen Industry* was founded; later it was affiliated to the Guild of St George. In the market town of Keswick in Cumberland there are relics devoted to Ruskin in this connection.

On Ruskin's death, February 8th, 1900, workers of the Linen Industry, under the direction of Miss Twelves, paid him their last homage. They worked day and night to weave a pall of linen, lined with rich rose silk. On the linen they embroidered their emblem and Ruskin's favourite flower – the wild rose – together with the inscription 'Unto this last'.

Of the eight individual linen industries in the Lake District only one now remains: The Flax Home Industry, in the picturesque village of Grasmere, established some sixty years ago. The Studio still displays Greek lace worked by elderly local embroideresses. A treasured exhibit is a letter of thanks together with a duplicate pincushion accepted by Her Majesty the Queen on the occasion of her wedding.

These people in the Lake District who, over the last half-century, have fostered this age-old craft, by teaching and by learning, have retained the high quality of a creative art, always aiming at perfection (PLATE 15); designs such as those illustrated in Plates 16, 17, 18 and 19 which were handed down from one worker to another and were used in the past on frills and furbelows, have now been adapted to grace the homes, in particular the table, of the twentieth century (PLATES 19 and 20).

CHAPTER III

Development of Open-work

FOR the embroideress who prefers to stitch freely over her fabric, rather than being confined to a traced line, counted thread embroidery offers a wealth of opportunity and variety in stitch and design. Under this heading many styles of embroidery come to mind: canvas work, Assisi embroidery, Black work, and Cross stitch, to mention a few. Then there is Pulled Fabric embroidery (sometimes called Drawn Fabric), perhaps the first step towards true open-work, because the pulled stitches give the material a lacy appearance though all the threads of the fabric remain intact (*fig 2*).

Open-work may be defined as drawn-thread work (*punto tirato*), in which the threads are drawn out *one* way only, either the warp or the weft; and cut-work (*punto tagliato*) in which the threads are drawn *both* ways, the warp and the weft, then cut to leave an empty space. Drawn-work is one of the oldest forms of embroidery, dating back to early times when it is believed that the fine linen vestments and altar linen were entirely ornamented by delicate patterns worked over the drawn threads. Many countries of Europe as well as those farther east influenced the characteristic lace-like borders and shapes achieved by darning and overcasting the undrawn warp and weft threads. As will be appreciated after studying the following step-by-step instructions, drawn-thread work is the link between pulled fabric embroidery and cut-work, all three being classed as open-work. Drawn-thread work by tradition has always been embroidered on white or natural linen with self-coloured thread (*fig 3*).

The basic form of hem-stitching shown in *figure* 4 may be adapted into several styles. First by varying the grouping of the threads in the space of the drawn threads: *Ladder Hem-stitch:* the hem-stitch is worked along both edges of the space of the drawn threads (*fig 5*). *Zig-Zag Hem-stitch:* in the first row there is an even number of threads in each group; in the second row the groups are made up of half the number

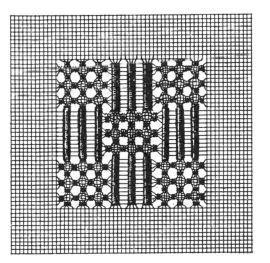

Fig 2   Pulled Fabric Embroidery

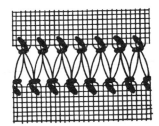

Fig 3   Drawn-Thread Work

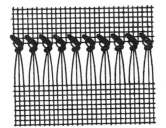

Fig 4   Hem-stitching

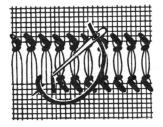

Fig 5   Ladder Hem-stitch

Fig 6   Zig-zag Hem-stitch

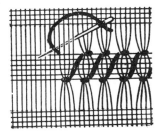

Fig 7a

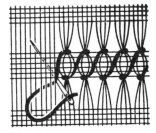

Fig 7b

Double or Italian Hem-stitch

of threads from one group and half from the adjacent group (*fig* 6). *Double* or *Italian Hem-stitch* is worked over two sets of drawn threads (*figs* 7 *a* and *b*).

A second way of ornamenting the space of drawn threads is to interlace a new thread along the groups of threads already made; the interlacing thread may also be knotted round the interlaced groups (*figs* 8 and 9).

Another method is to overcast or weave the threads into 'Bars', very characteristic of Hardanger embroidery, but also used in drawn-thread work (*figs* 10 A and B). These bars form the main foundation structure of the cut-work designs seen in this book.

In linen cut-work the Open-Hem (see Sampler 1, PLATE 21) is a variation of drawn-work. Each open-hem stitch is worked over a square of four threads, along two sets of two drawn threads with four undrawn threads between. This open-hem plays a very important part in linen cut-work; it is frequently worked immediately below the turned-down hem, or as an independent decorative design, and nearly always as a framework for the cut-out area, whatever the shape or size (*fig* 18).

The empty spaces, caused by drawing threads both ways of the material, first appeared in the corners of drawn-thread designs. The loose ends drawn back into the corners were either pushed back into the hem-turning or darned into the surrounding fabric (*fig* 11), the raw edges of the corners being neatened by buttonhole stitch, and the empty square then filled with some kind of open-work decoration such as a spider's web.

In the earliest samples of cut-work the raw edges were neatened by an overcast stitch whipped over additional loose threads laid along the raw edge to form a strong cording (*fig* 12) so essential as an anchorage for the cut-out fillings (see *The Padded Roll*, Chapter IV and *fig* 19).

Following the stage of 'empty corners' introduced in drawn-thread embroidery, more warp and weft threads were deliberately cut instead of being drawn right through to make blank spaces in the background material (*fig* 13).

The trellised pattern of undrawn threads and open spaces governed the early cut-work designs; the interlacing threads were worked into rolls and bars and the blank spaces were filled with simple outlines (see *fig* 14). Gradually more and more threads were drawn out until the only threads to remain undrawn are those which mark the centre each way across the cut-out area, as described in Chapter IV, *figure* 17.

The bold geometric designs of the fifteenth century developed into the lace-like appearance of early needle-point lace of the sixteenth century. The introduction of *couronnes* (tiny loops) buttonholed over the foundation threads and the 'bobs' (twisted knots made into loops) all helped to break up and lighten the designs. A

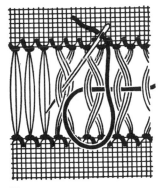

Fig 8

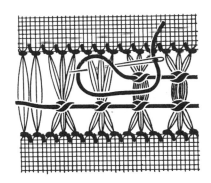

Fig 9

Figs 8 *and* 9   Interlacing

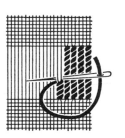

Fig 10*a*   Overcast Bars

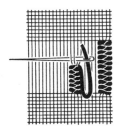

Fig 10*b*   Woven Bars

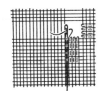

Fig 11 Corner Neatening

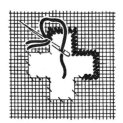

Fig 12   Raw Edges

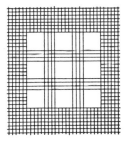

Fig 13   Cut Threads

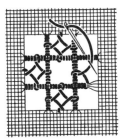

Fig 14   Bars and Fillings

little later, attractive lozenge shapes were woven or worked into buttonhole stitch along the foundation threads (*figs* 26 and 27).

Figures 15 and 16 show two interesting cut-work designs from specimen embroideries housed in the Victoria and Albert Museum. The inside of the petals and leaf of the flower motif have been cut out in *figure* 15, the raw edges neatened with a narrow cording and the stem and scalloped 'trailings' worked in overcast stitch. *Figure* 16 is typical of the fancy motifs, embroidered in satin stitch, frequently interspersed with cut-out designs.

Fig 15

Fig 16

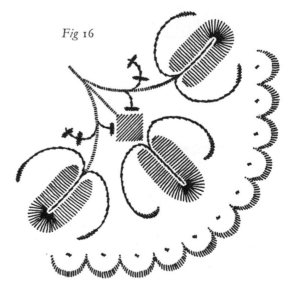

PLATE 13 THE SPINNERS' GALLERY AT CONISTON

PLATE 14   CORNER WORKED IN RUSKIN LINEN WORK BY AUTHOR

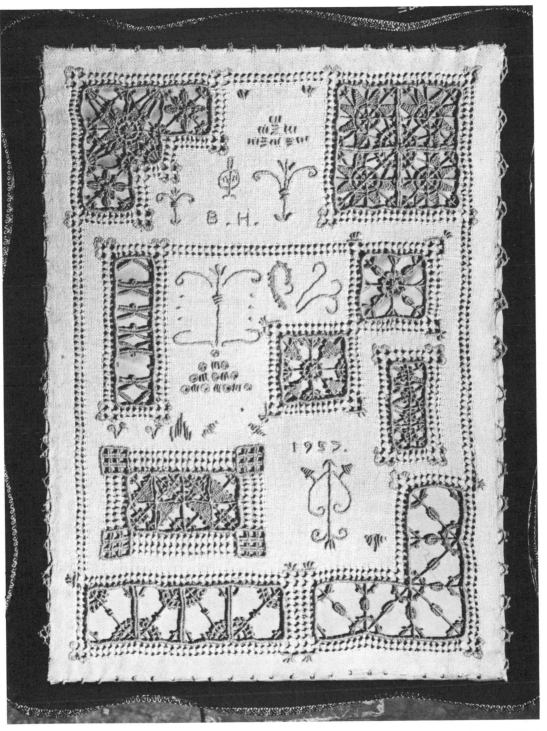

PLATE 15   SAMPLER WORKED IN GREEK LACE BY MRS
BETTY HODGSON, GRANGE-OVER-SANDS (*see also
Samplers I and II, Plates* 21 *and* 22)

PLATE 16   A TRADITIONAL LAVENDER BAG BY AUTHOR

PLATE 17   A BOX AND PINCUSHION BY AUTHOR

PLATE 18   PART OF A TRAY CLOTH WORKED BY AUTHOR

PLATE 19   A TABLE SET IN FINE ITALIAN LINEN BY AUTHOR

PLATE 20   TABLE NAPKIN (*corner detail of napkin in Plate* 19)
WORKED IN FINE ITALIAN HAND-MADE LINEN
BY AUTHOR

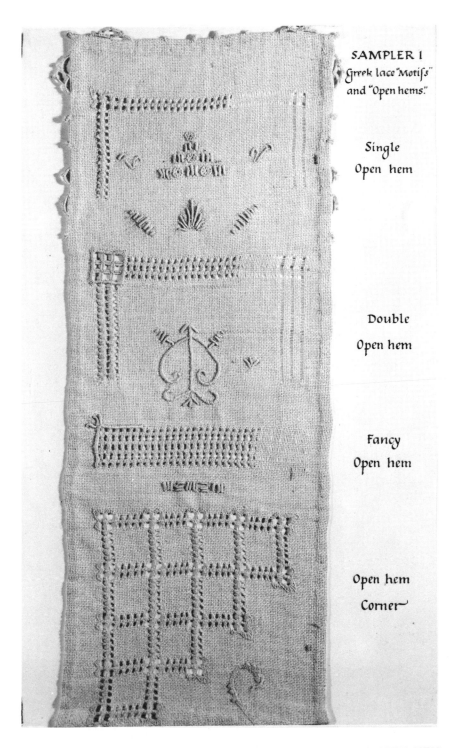

SAMPLER I
Greek lace "Motifs"
and "Open hems."

Single
Open hem

Double
Open hem

Fancy
Open hem

Open hem
Corner

PLATE 21   SAMPLER I — GREEK LACE MOTIFS AND OPEN-HEM

PLATE 22   SAMPLER II – WORKING AN EDGING BY AUTHOR

PLATE 23   CHURCH AND STEEPLE, BY MISS MARION PRIOR,
GOLDSMITHS' SCHOOL OF ART

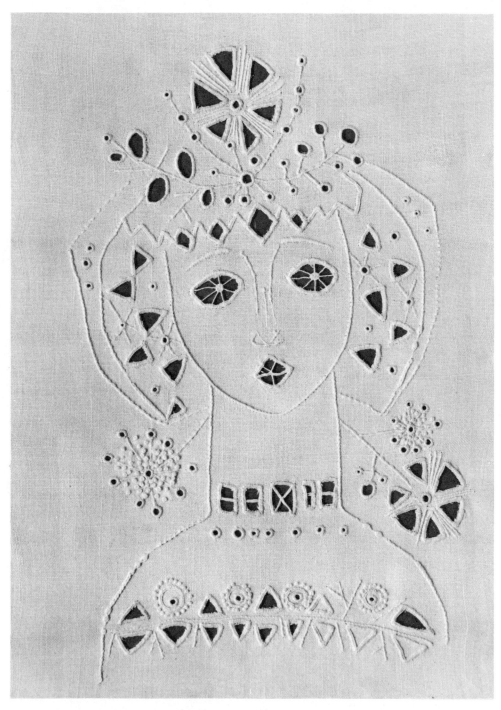

PLATE 24   A HEAD, WORKED ON WHITE LINEN WITH A
BLUE BACKGROUND, BY SISTER PETRONA, GOLD-
SMITHS' SCHOOL OF ART

CHAPTER IV

The Foundation Structure of Cut-Work

DRAWING OUT THE THREADS (*fig* 17)

WHEN planning a pattern, whatever the shape, the calculations to be considered are: the dimensions of the cut-out area, and the type of open-hem to be worked.

If the open-work is designed to fill a square, the threads must be counted on the material, as well as being measured, each side of the square, so as to ensure perfect symmetry.

With the help of pins to mark the threads, draw a single thread round the outside of the cut-out area (see letter A). First cut the thread in the middle of the length to be drawn, unpick and draw it back to the corner and then cut it there.

Find the middle thread each way of the square, mark it with a pin, leave a thread on either side of it, draw out a single thread adjacent to these, so as to isolate three threads vertically and horizontally across the centre of the square (see letter B). This makes four small squares, which are to be cut out after the padded roll has been worked.

The four threads immediately outside the square must be left undrawn (see letter C). These four threads will be worked over as the padded roll.

The width of the open-hem depends on whether a single or double open-hem is to be worked; for a single open-hem (see letter D) two threads are drawn, four threads left and two more threads drawn. For a double open-hem (see letter E) a further four threads are left and two more threads drawn.

This method of drawing the threads is followed whether the pattern is a simple square or a more complicated piece of insertion. It is advisable to plan the pattern on graph paper before drawing the threads of the material.

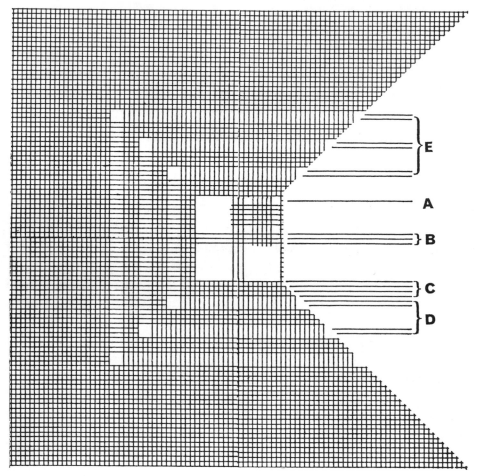

Fig 17   Drawing out the threads

THE OPEN-HEM (*fig* 18)

As already mentioned in the previous chapter, an open-hem is worked as a framework round the 'lace' pattern; whether a single or double open-hem is chosen, the open-hem is always stitched first, before the work is attached to the temporary backing of leather-cloth.

The open-hem may be the only decoration on a piece of work; by varying the drawn threads and the threads left undrawn, some interesting combinations can be achieved (Open-Hem Sampler 1, PLATE 21).

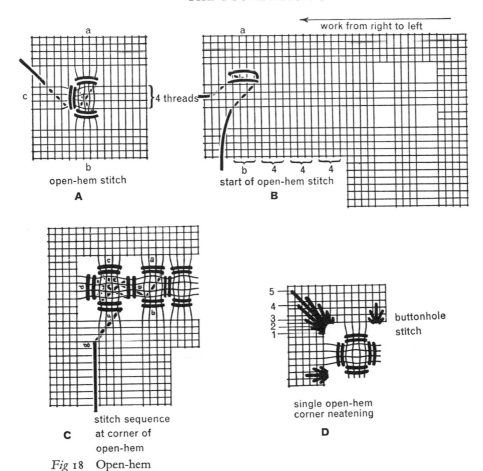

Fig 18   Open-hem

The open-hem stitch (*fig* 18 A) is worked in the same way for all types of open-hem. One point that has to be noted is that some lines may be worked over twice; first from below, then from round the four threads in question (A or B in stitch diagram). In this case the thread is taken round the four threads once only when working each line, instead of twice.

To start the open-hem stitch (*fig* 18 B), work from right to left and keep the first loose end under the thumb until it has been caught in by the first few stitches; all other ends can be neatened off into the back of the open-hem work. The sequence of the stitches at the corners is best explained by *figure* 18 C. The single and double open-hem each have their own particular 'corner' neatening, to prevent the holes

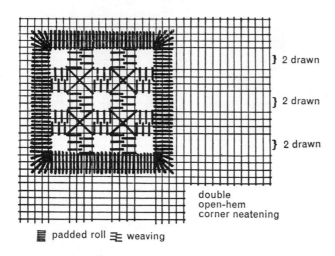

} 2 drawn

} 2 drawn

} 2 drawn

double
open-hem
corner neatening

▤ padded roll ╪ weaving

E.

Fig 18   Open-hem

(formed by drawing and cutting the threads each way of the material) becoming frayed.

The three holes round the outside of a single open-hem are neatened by a series of buttonhole stitches worked over 1, 2, 3, 2, 1, threads into the first hole, then over 1, 2, 3, 4, 5, 4, 3, 2, 1, threads into the corner hole, and then the third hole is worked in the same way as the first (*fig* 18 D).

The neatening of the double open-hem is rather more complicated; small weavings are worked inside the square formed at the 'corners'. First a padded roll is worked (*fig* 18 E) over two padding threads, round the outside of the square; cut out two of the threads in each group of four inside the square (replace them by two threads of the working linen thread). With the working linen thread weave across the four threads from one side of the square to the other. Where the fabric threads meet take the weaving thread diagonally across so that a small cross is formed at each junction.

THE PADDED ROLL (*fig* 19)

As is so often the case in any craft, the most tedious part of linen cut-work is by far the most important preparation and guarantee to a satisfactory finished result: the padded roll. To make a success of any pattern it cannot be over-emphasised that the greatest possible care must be taken in working this roll; it has to carry the whole foundation scaffolding, on to which the lacy fillings are ultimately attached.

When drawing the threads, four threads were left undrawn between the cut-out

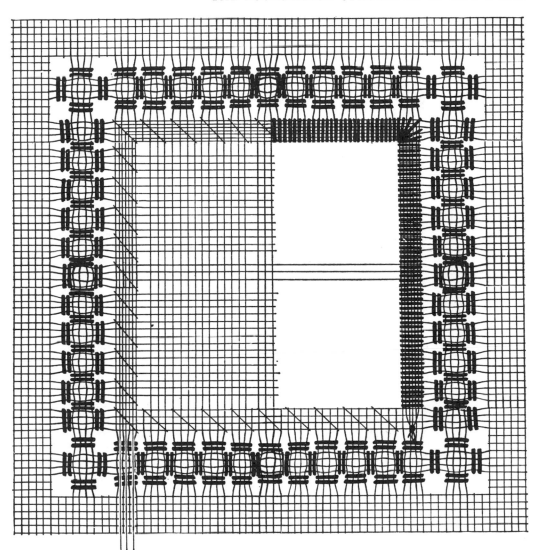

Fig 19   Padded Roll

area and the open hem (*fig* 17 C); it is on to these four threads that the padded roll is worked.

Using a rather thicker thread than that used for the open-hem, overcast the four threads with stitches to take in approximately the width of each open-hem hole, round the four sides of the square.

Fig 20

From the same working thread cut three lengths, each long enough to go round the overcast square (allowing a little more thread than the exact measurement); knot the three threads together. These become the padding threads of the padded roll.

Start at one corner and lay the three loose threads on to the four overcast threads; with a new working thread whip over and over, in very closely packed stitches, both the overcast stitches and the loose padding threads. Keep the latter under the thumb as the whipping proceeds.

The stitches should be so close to each other that no gaps appear; after a few stitches the knot joining the loose threads together may be pulled up firmly against the first whipping stitches. It is important to keep an even tension of stitch: the roll does not want to become so tightly pulled that it appears rope-like, yet it must be firm enough not to be disturbed by the needle and thread passing through it in several places when other threads are secured to it. The stitches round the corners need to be pushed up well into the corner so that each corner is square and not rounded. When the last corner is reached cut off the knot and the surplus ends of the loose padding threads and neaten off with a few more whipped stitches.

THE FOUNDATION THREADS (*fig* 20)

When the padded roll is completed and the four small inner squares are cut out, cut along the padded roll as close as possible to the whipping stitches. Care must be taken not to cut the three threads which were left undrawn across the centre of the square in both directions.

All the main foundation threads, whether overcast rolls or woven bars, are secured through the padded roll. The first horizontal and vertical threads always remain on top, and all other foundation threads are brought in below however many foundation threads are added.

It is most important to keep the foundation threads even in all directions. A constant check with a small piece of paper and a tape-measure is necessary, otherwise the pattern is easily thrown out of balance.

The three threads left undrawn across the cut-out area tend to stretch, so that it is necessary to add further strands of the working thread to give support. If an overcast roll is worked, one of the three undrawn threads is cut out, then two further threads are added through the padded roll, making four in all. If the three threads are to be worked into a woven bar, then three extra threads are added, giving six threads to weave over (*figs* 21 and 22).

The main diagonal foundation threads, worked as rolls, over three threads are secured into the corners of the padded roll.

All other foundation bars and rolls are attached to this first main foundation structure; these with the build-up of the lace forms and stitches construct each pattern.

CHAPTER V

Stitches

THE main foundation bars and rolls of any cut-out pattern must be carefully laid and worked over before the 'lace' fillings are added. Special care should be exerted in making sure that this first foundation structure is executed with attention to the positioning of the foundation threads and the uniformity of the stitches worked over them.

THE WEAVE STITCH (*fig* 21)

The woven bars are made up of four or six foundation threads worked over with a weave stitch.

For the two main bars across the centre of the cut-out area three additional foundation threads must be laid with the three undrawn threads; pull the added threads a little tighter than the undrawn threads. Other woven bars are worked over four or six foundation threads.

With the same working thread as that used for laying the foundation threads, start weaving over three threads and under three. Continue in this manner right up the bar; each stitch should touch the last. Make sure the tension is even so that the bar is the same width all the way.

At the central point (which should be accurately measured) take a single stitch across the junction of the two bars, making a cross where the two woven bars meet.

THE ROLL STITCH (*fig* 22)

The main vertical and horizontal foundation threads can also be worked into rolls; these need four foundation threads (one of the undrawn threads is cut out and two are added). Diagonal and other rolls are stitched over three foundation threads.

An overcast stitch is whipped over and over the foundation threads; each stitch

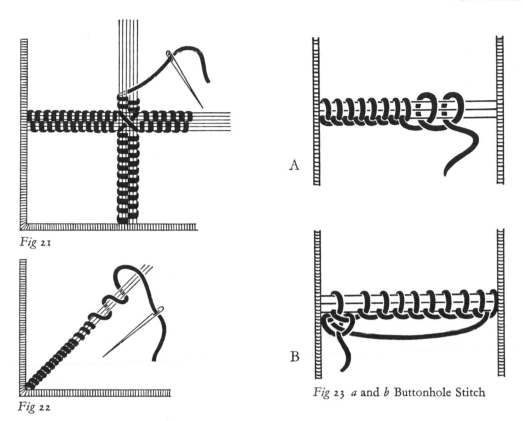

Fig 21

Fig 22

A

B

Fig 23 *a* and *b* Buttonhole Stitch

should be packed tightly against the last, so that there are no gaps. The stitches should not appear loose; nor, on the other hand, should the roll be too string-like: every stitch should be clearly definable.

THE BUTTONHOLE STITCH (*fig* 23)

When the main woven bar and the rolls have been completed the subsidiary button-hole bars should be worked.

The buttonholing (*fig* 23 A) is worked over three foundation threads laid in the required shape and position to form lines, circles, half-circles, squares and triangle effects. Keep the stitches close together so that a solid, even buttonholed bar is made.

The first row of buttonhole stitches can be extended to form solid shapes, such as 'points' and 'petals', by decreasing or increasing the stitches at the beginning and end of each row. A single foundation thread is carried back from the last stitch of each row up into the loop of the first stitch of that row; the next row of buttonholing is worked into the heading of the previous row, taking in the single foundation thread (*fig* 23 B). When working a circle of petals over three foundation threads care should be taken to work the same number of buttonhole stitches in the first row for each petal (that is, between each foundation roll or bar).

After completing a point, the sides can be neatened and the shape improved by overcasting from row to row down the side; or if picots are to be added, neaten in the same way with buttonhole stitch.

Interesting additions to the lace structure of the cut-out patterns can be obtained by working the rolls and buttonhole bars in conjunction, as is done in the Heavy Bar and the Open Bar.

THE HEAVY BAR (*fig* 24)

This is most often worked as a circle or a square.

The three foundation threads are first secured through the connecting rolls and bars, and a roll is completed (*fig* 24 A). Then carry back a single foundation thread up into the start of the roll; with this thread start a series of buttonhole stitches along the roll (*fig* 24 B). The spacing of the stitches depends on whether buttonholing is to be worked over the roll from one side only, or from both; if from both sides, the space left between each stitch when working the first side must be just enough to be neatly filled by one single stitch (which will be made when working the second side).

If an even heavier bar is required, after completing the first row of buttonhole stitches another single foundation thread can be carried back into the first stitch of that row, and a second row of buttonholing worked into the heading of the previous row (*fig* 24 C).

The same procedure that is shown in *figure* 24 B and C is followed when working the second side of the roll, either with one or two rows of buttonhole stitches.

THE OPEN BAR (*fig* 25)

The open bar is comprised of a roll and a buttonhole bar joined at intervals by a twisted thread carried from the buttonholing down round the roll and back again.

First work the roll round three foundation threads; then attach three foundation threads for the buttonhole bar. The space between the roll and the bar will vary according to the pattern; it is usually about an eighth to a quarter of an inch (*fig* 25 A).

Start working buttonhole stitches along the foundation threads in the usual way.

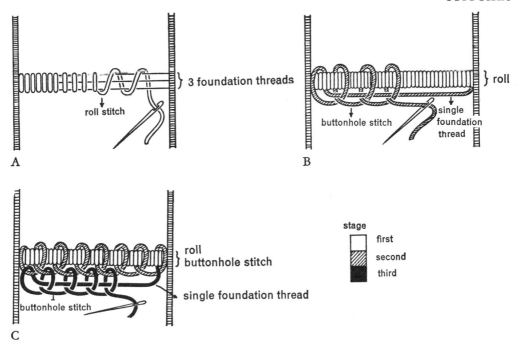

A

B

C

Fig 24   Buttonhole Bars

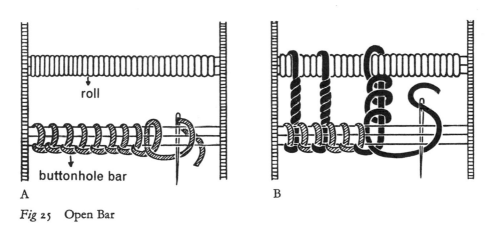

A

B

Fig 25   Open Bar

To join the roll and the bar take the needle under the bar, and round behind the roll; pull up the thread to the width required between the roll and the bar. Twist the needle three times round the single cross thread, and back into the last stitch of the buttonholing; pull up the thread through the twists, holding them gently between finger and thumb; and continue buttonholing.

Like the heavy bar the open bar is most often worked as a square or a full circle.

LOZENGES

After the main and subsidiary rolls, weaves and buttonhole bars have been worked, as well as extensions and variations on them, a further ornamentation of lozenges, knots and picots are added. These give the fillings a more lacy appearance; they also add considerable interest to the structure of the designs.

There are two styles of lozenge: one is worked in buttonhole stitch, while the other is woven. They are best placed on to the rolls.

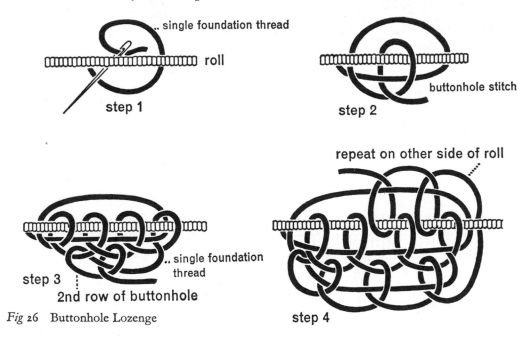

Fig 26   Buttonhole Lozenge

Buttonhole Lozenge (*fig* 26). Secure the end of the thread in the roll. Take a single foundation thread down, through, and back along the roll to form a lozenge of the required size (Step 1).

Work a row of buttonhole stitches along the roll, taking in the foundation thread (Step 2). Space the stitches so that there is sufficient room for another stitch between each, on the opposite side of the lozenge.

At the end of the first row of buttonhole stitches take another single thread back to the start of the first row and work a second row of buttonholing into the previous row (Step 3).

At the end of the second row, work one stitch over the roll, turn the work round and repeat Steps 2 and 3 on the other side of the lozenge (Step 4).

Woven Lozenge (*fig* 27). Having decided the size of the lozenge, secure the working thread into the roll and carry three foundation threads through the roll. Continuing with the same working thread weave over the three foundation threads on the one side of the roll, under the roll, and over the second set of three threads (*fig* 27 A);

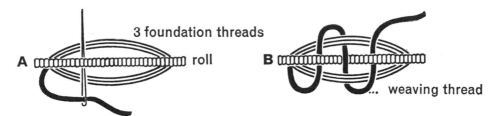

Fig 27   Woven Lozenge

work back under the foundation threads and over the roll (*fig* 27 B), and continue this weaving pattern.

Pack the stitches well up into the ends of the lozenge, and make the stitches a little looser in the centre to give extra width to the lozenge shape.

KNOTS

Knots, both bullion and picot, are very characteristic of linen cut-work. The bullion knots may be worked over the rolls and across the bars; they may also be worked where the foundation threads meet in the centre of a pattern. The picots are dropped off buttonholed shapes such as points and petals; they are also interspersed along the buttonhole bars.

Bullion Knot (*fig* 28 A). As shown in Chapter VII, there are several ways of grouping bullion knots; they may be worked singly, in pairs, or in groups of three; for the latter two knots are worked side by side, and the third goes through the loops of the other two knots and surmounts them.

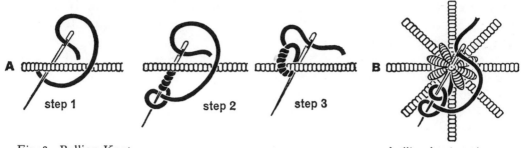

Fig 28   Bullion Knot

bullion knot centre

To work the bullion knot, secure the working thread into the roll or bar at the point where the knot is to be placed; bring the thread out through the bottom of the roll and round it, as if starting a buttonhole stitch (Step 1). Twist the needle a number of times anticlockwise round the thread close to where it comes out of the roll (Step 2). The number of twists will govern the size of the knot. Keeping the twists held gently between thumb and finger, draw the needle and thread through them (stroke the twists with a needle inserted into the loop of the knot, so that the twists draw up tightly to the base of the roll or bar). Secure the bullion knot in its place with a stitch into the roll or bar (Step 3).

A Bullion Knot Centre (*fig* 28 B) consists of a series of bullion knots worked between the foundation threads where the bars and rolls meet. For each knot the needle should be brought out of and inserted into a common central point. Twelve twists are taken round the needle for each bullion knot.

Fig 29   Picot Knot

A Picot Knot (*fig* 29) is worked off any buttonhole stitch. Make a second buttonhole stitch into the last loop made (Step 1). Insert the needle through the loop of the buttonhole stitch just made (Step 2). Twist the working thread round the needle (Step 3). Draw up the knot and pass the needle through the loop of the original buttonhole stitch (Step 4), ready to continue the buttonholing. As the knot is pulled up into place it twists itself into a neat little coronet.

CHAPTER VI

The Design

FROM an extensive study of pattern books, some of which date back to the earliest stages of linen cut-work, it is interesting to note that it is the design which has changed over the centuries rather than the technique. When looking in the books from Italy or in the valuable records now in the library of the Victoria and Albert Museum, one particular characteristic of cut-work stands out: the easy flow and the continuity of design. This is so whether the design is a single square or a more elaborate combination of shapes. The eye is never conscious of one separate unit in the design; it is led from one part to another to appreciate the pattern as a whole. If the pattern is taken apart, one usually finds that each unit is a perfect design in itself – or could easily be adapted into such. Throughout the centuries the patterns have tended to remain geometrical in style, with a bold simplicity of stitch, and no colour. The contrasts depend on balance and proportion for their effect.

It is very important to make the lace fillings sufficiently concentrated inside the cut-out area so as not to give an empty appearance; yet to over-fill is also a mistake. Each form must be free and clear. When the student has had practice in reproducing some of the patterns given for working the simpler 2-inch squares she will have become acquainted with various forms, or combinations of forms, built up from the stitches of the previous chapter. It is then quite possible to adapt the designs into further original patterns.

It is essential to be quite sure that a pleasing and well-balanced design has been achieved before any stitching is added. It is also important to consider how to use the pattern: the weight of thread for working the stitches, and the type of material to use. No amount of expert stitching will correct a poor design, so it is wise to draw the design on to a piece of sectional paper the same shape and size as the pattern to be worked; then place the pattern template into position on the material. This

will help to plan the open-hem framework and further decoration. It is too late to have second thoughts once the threads have been drawn. No time given in planning is ever lost, especially in this type of work where a considerable amount of stitching is done in a small space.

The patterns shown on pages 62–67 are either traditional, or adapted from the many designs passed from one worker to another. Over a number of generations

this pooling of resources by interested workers has been the only means of acquiring patterns, so it is impossible to tell where any one pattern originated; but it is safe to say that many of these patterns have enjoyed a long history. This is clearly illustrated by comparing the photographs of surviving samples shown in this book.

The size and shape of the design must be largely governed by the use to be made of it, but many of the patterns can be reduced or enlarged to suit a specific require-

ment. A design given to fill a 2-inch cut-out area is perhaps the most useful, because this can easily be adapted into more elaborate combinations. Other designs to suit a 'centre piece', a 'corner' or an 'insertion' are also to be found on pages 65–67. The various stitches are given in detail in Chapter V, but the following short résumé may be of help. Each design is best worked from the centre outwards.

The first horizontal and vertical foundation threads together with the diagonal

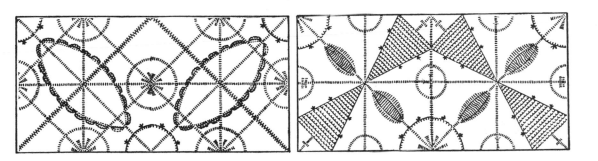

foundation threads are worked over into either rolls or woven bars (*figs* 21 and 22).

The 'centres' are worked with a series of bullion knots, each of twelve twists, between each foundation, or woven into a cobweb; the thread being carried over and under the foundation rolls, five complete turns give a pleasing effect (*fig* 28 B).

Further foundation structure is added by rolls worked over three foundation threads, in the form of squares, circles or half-circles. The same three threads may also be worked with buttonhole stitches (*fig* 23 A).

65

Points and petals are accomplished by following the buttonhole stitch and extension (*fig* 23). The first line of buttonholing is worked over three foundation threads; the subsequent lines are worked over a single foundation thread taken back from the previous row, and into the buttonhole stitch of the last row worked. The form required is achieved by the addition or reduction of the number of stitches in each row. The raw edges of the point and petal are drawn further into shape and neatened by overcasting into each end stitch, taking the thread from one row to the next.

The predominating squares and circles are worked in the heavy bar; a roll worked over in buttonhole stitch, and a further line of buttonholing worked into the first. This is carried out on both sides of the roll (*fig* 24). As an alternative the open bar can be used: again a combination of the roll and buttonhole bar joined by a twisted thread (*fig* 25).

An embellishment of knots and picots is an essential part of linen cut-work. These are either worked over the rolls as bullion knots, or completed from any buttonhole stitch as picots (*fig* 29).

Lozenge shapes, aptly called 'bugs', are worked along the rolls; these may be woven or buttonholed (*figs* 26 and 27).

Fig 30   Motifs and Edgings

CHAPTER VII

Motifs and Edgings

MOTIFS (*fig* 30)

THESE are an attractive addition to the traditional Greek Lace; the motifs are embroidered on the linen interspersed with the open-work; they are worked with one strand of the same thread as that used for the fillings. They can be embroidered in varying ways according to the shape and size. Long bullion knots (*fig* 31 B) predominate; these are the only decoration in D, F, G and L; while they are combined with eyelets in B.

The trailing lines in A are first worked in a single line of close running stitches, which are then overcast into thin outlines (*fig* 31 A). Pick up as small an amount of

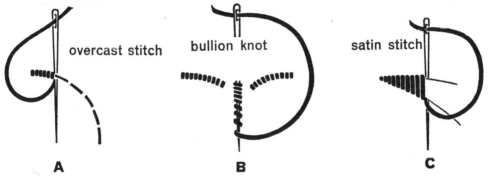

overcast stitch   bullion knot   satin stitch

A   **B**   **C**

Fig 31   Embroidery Stitches

background material as possible with each stitch, so that the raised line has a rounded look. The shaded tips are covered with satin stitch laid in an oblique direction (*fig* 31 C).

In C the three lines are again traced in running stitches which are then overcast. Small bullion knots are added at the points.

E, H and K are embroidered in a similar manner; the long bullion knots are splayed across the overcast lines, and the smaller knots complete the balance of the design.

A row of double buttonhole stitch is worked over the foundation of running stitches which outline the scroll of J; small picots dropped off the buttonhole stitches at regular intervals make another interesting decoration.

BUTTONHOLE AND KNOT EDGINGS (*fig* 32)

All pieces of linen cut-work, whether large or small, should include the characteristic edging of bullion knots or buttonhole loops; these are embroidered along the edges of the hem. On small articles, such as a needle-book, trinket box, pincushion or bag, the bullion knots are used to join the various pieces together. On table linen the knots and loops serve as an extra ornament.

As will be seen in the sampler of knots and loops in *figure* 32, there are several adaptations of both. Each bullion knot (A) is worked right through the edge of the hem turning; these may be single knots, or pairs. The pairs may also have another bullion knot across the top; that is, the knot is worked through the two loops of the pair of knots, so no material is taken up. The number of times the working thread is twisted round the needle governs the size of the knot; for knots worked as an edging ten or twelve twists are usually required.

To vary the loops worked in buttonhole stitch (C), a foundation of three threads is needed (D). Take the working thread from (a) to (b) – i.e. right to left – back to (a), then once more to (b), so that the buttonhole stitch can be worked from left to right over the three foundation threads. E shows a slightly more complicated loop formation: after taking the three foundation threads from (a) to (b) as before, the buttonholing is worked over the first loop and half the second, as far as (c). From here a third loop is added on to the top of the first two, before completing the buttonhole stitch of the second loop back to (a).

Picots added to the buttonhole stitches when working the loops give an attractive finish (B).

PUNTO-IN-ARIA (*fig* 33)

An edging of punto-in-aria, which is built up on the same principle of forms and stitches as the cut-work designs, must be included here, since Greek Lace and punto-in-aria are so often found together. As we said in Chapter I, linen cut-work cannot be neatly defined as 'lace' or 'embroidery'; but certainly this edging of punto-

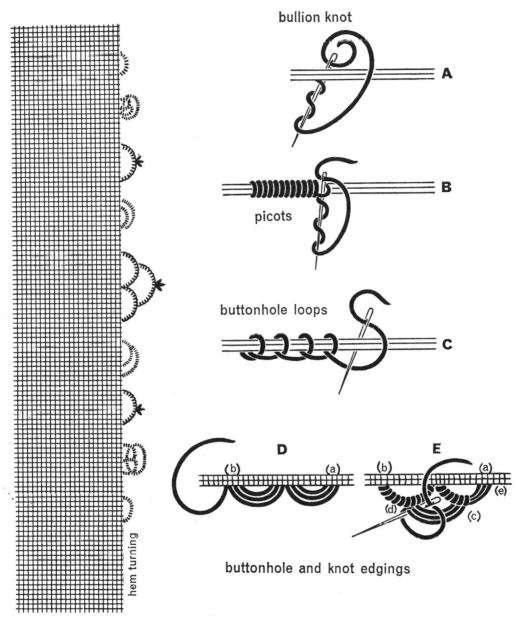

bullion knot

A

picots

B

buttonhole loops

C

D

(b)   (a)

E

(b)   (a)

(e)

(d)   (c)

buttonhole and knot edgings

hem turning

Fig 32

in-aria comes nearest to lace, for the only connection between the edging and the material is the padded roll (see Sampler 2, PLATE 22).

The design for the edging is first drawn on to the white side of oil-cloth – the modern replacement for the parchment used in the sixteenth century. This temporary foundation is then attached to the linen along the padded roll. It is important to stress here that the padded roll should be made with meticulous care.

From the padded roll the main foundation threads are laid along the corresponding lines (B and D) of the design on the oil-cloth, and anchored down on to it with a couple of stitches. These foundation threads are then worked into woven bars or rolls, as described in Chapter IV (*fig* 20).

To this first scaffolding more rolls and buttonholed bars may be added (C), before building up the patterns (E and F) with designs in buttonhole stitch and an embellishment of knots and picots. This is similar to the way the designs were created in the cut-out squares. A second edging of buttonholed loops (G) can be added.

When the whole edging has been completed the small anchoring stitches can be released (cut from behind the oil-cloth). The lace will fall away as the name suggests – free as air!

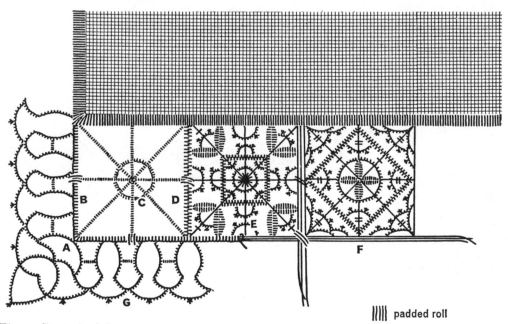

||||| padded roll

Fig 33   Punto-in-Aria

CHAPTER VIII

Adapting Small Designs

IN bygone days, the sampler appears to have been the introduction to any special-
ised type of embroidery. Nowadays, while the initial mastery of the technique
may still have to be boring, it is quite possible to practise on small useful pieces
of work from the start (see PLATES 16 and 17).

This chapter is designed to give the student ideas, to teach her linen cut-work and
at the same time to adapt even the first results into attractive articles such as a
needle-book, a napkin ring or a trinket box, or rather more ambitious projects
planned to make up into cushion covers and guest towels. Measurements and working instructions are given for a needle-book (see PLATE 1), a napkin ring and a box
or pincushion. Since the shape of the finished pincushion must necessarily determine
the layout and design employed, a set of guest towels gives more scope to try out
narrow insertion patterns.

THE NEEDLE-BOOK (*fig* 34 and PLATE 1)

The following materials are required:
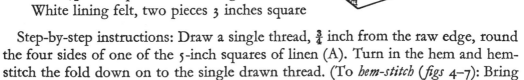

    Two 5-inch squares of evenweave linen
    One skein of linen lace thread, No. 35
    Two pieces of coloured lining silk
    Two 4½-inch squares of stiff cardboard
    Two 4½-inch squares of wadding
    White lining felt, two pieces 3 inches square

Step-by-step instructions: Draw a single thread, ¾ inch from the raw edge, round
the four sides of one of the 5-inch squares of linen (A). Turn in the hem and hem-
stitch the fold down on to the single drawn thread. (To *hem-stitch* (*figs* 4–7): Bring

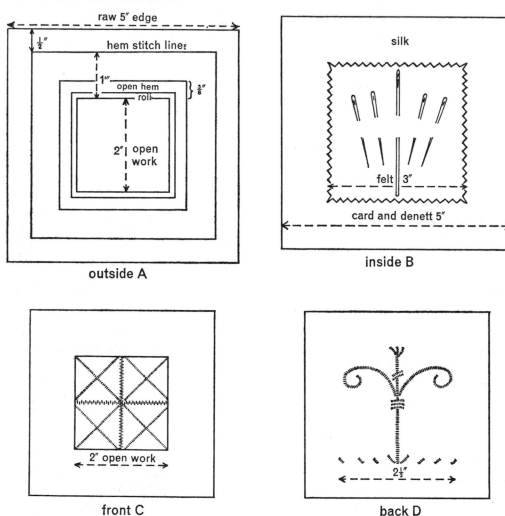

Fig 34

the working thread out to the right of the first threads to be worked over. Pass the needle behind the loose threads twice; the second time bring the needle through the very edge of the hem turning. The number of threads taken up in each stitch must vary according to the weight of the linen.) Draw a single thread round the 2-inch centre square, 1 inch inside the hem-stitching. Leaving four threads outside this square for the padded roll (*fig* 19), draw the threads for a single open-hem. Work the open-hem and padded roll as described in *figure* 18.

Select a 2-inch design and work it in the cut-out square (see patterns, pages 62–63), to complete the front cover of the needle-book. Embroider the motif shown in *figure* 30 K, to fill a 2-inch square on the back cover (*fig* 34 D).

With both covers of the book completed, make up as follows: Place a square of wadding on one side of each piece of card, with the silk on the other side. Fold the raw edges of the silk over the card, on to the wadding. Fit these two lots of card, wadding and silk lining to the completed lined front cover and back embroidered cover, and overcast all the pieces together with tacking stitches.

Work bullion knots (*fig* 28 A) to join the inside and the outside of the covers along three sides. Hinge the covers together with pairs of bullion knots (*fig* 43 A and B). Pink the edges of the felt needle carriers and attach in position inside the book (*fig* 34 B). Make a small flat cobweb button and attach it to the front cover, working a buttonhole loop over three foundation threads on the back cover to fasten the needle-book together (*fig* 43 D and E).

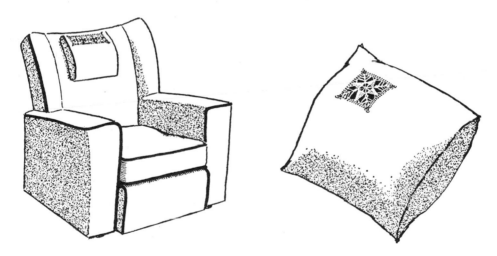

CUSHIONS of varying shapes and sizes present numerous opportunities for interesting layouts and the use of both large and small cut-work designs. As well as the traditional square cushion, there is the small modern oblong TV head pillow; and the popular scatter cushions do much to furnish a contemporary home. It is best to embroider the cut-out designs on to loose linen covers to fit over the coloured cushion; the cover of the cushion inside serves as a coloured background to the cut-work fillings.

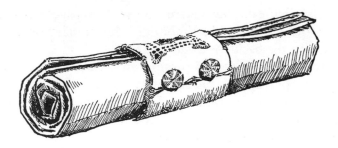

THE TABLE NAPKIN RING (*fig 35*)

A set of six table napkin rings gives ample scope for practice in working small insertion patterns; a wide choice of suitable designs may be found in Chapter VI. The following materials are needed for each of the rings:

> One 6-inch square of evenweave linen
> One skein of lace linen thread No. 35 to match or contrast with the linen
> A small piece of silk for lining behind the cut-out pattern

Figure 35 gives the actual measurements of each ring. A single thread is drawn round the size of the cut-out area, $3\frac{1}{2}$ inches by 1 inch, in the centre of the linen. Care needs to be taken in drawing out the threads for the open-hem; draw the threads *back* into the corners so that there is no pull on the threads beyond the cut-out area.

Divide up the $3\frac{1}{2}$ by 1 inch rectangle into three 1-inch squares; isolate each square by leaving three threads undrawn to become two vertical woven bars. Outside the cut-out area the padded roll is worked, also the open-hem framework; for these follow instructions in Chapter IV and *figures* 18 and 19. After working the woven bars D and E the other foundation threads are worked over as rolls; then complete the cut-out design with motifs and knots: for details of stitches see Chapter V.

Remove the temporary leather cloth backing and stitch the coloured silk lining into place, behind the cut-out area and the open-hem. The finished ring should measure 5 inches by $2\frac{1}{2}$ inches. Turn the surplus linen to the back of the ring and neaten it over the silk lining.

Work bullion knots at half-inch intervals along the top and bottom edges, then place two hand-made cobweb buttons, and corresponding loops worked in button-hole stitches, to fasten the ring (see *fig* 43 D and E). In place of the designs given in *figure* 35 any 1-inch patterns can be chosen to make up the insertion (see patterns, page 66).

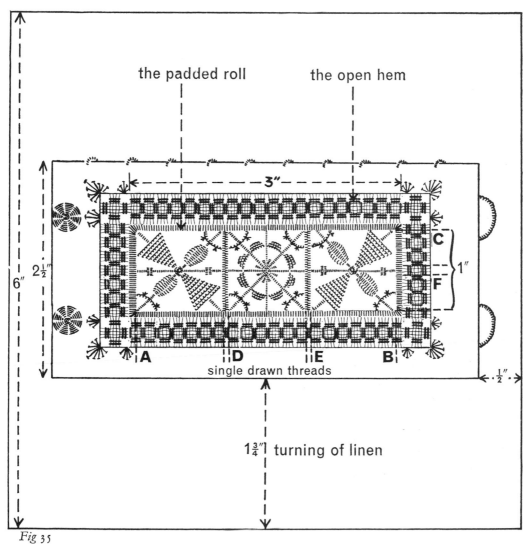

the padded roll   the open hem

3"

C

1"

F

2½"

6"

A D E B

single drawn threads

½"

1¾" turning of linen

Fig 35

PINCUSHIONS (*fig* 36 and PLATE 17) may be classed as rather old-fashioned but they still have their uses! They may be made any shape and size; the cut-out design should be chosen accordingly and worked on a loose linen cover. By tradition the little pillow made to fill the cover was stuffed with cedar wood, sweet-smelling as well as being excellent for the needles. Instructions for making a pincushion are shown in *figure* 36 C.

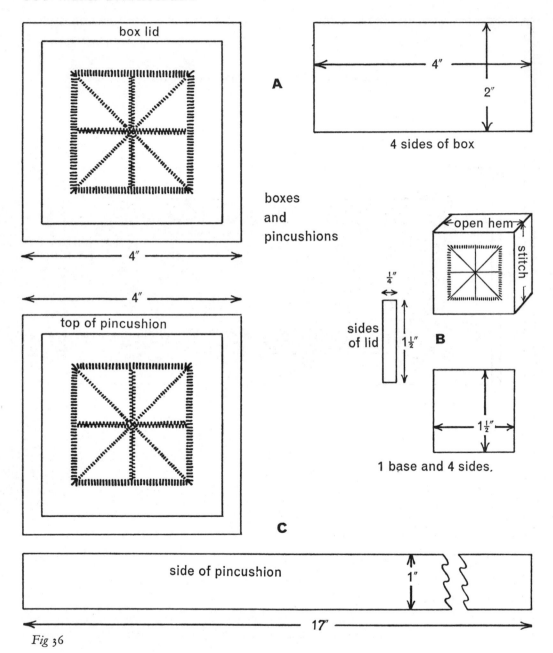

box lid

A

4"

2"

4 sides of box

boxes
and
pincushions

4"

4"

top of pincushion

open hem

stitch

B

sides
of lid

$\frac{1}{4}$"

$1\frac{1}{2}$"

$1\frac{1}{2}$"

1 base and 4 sides.

C

side of pincushion

1"

17"

Fig 36

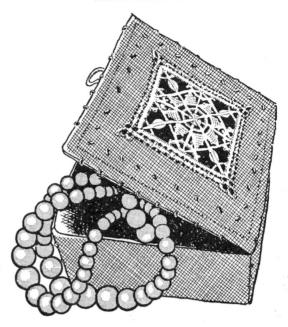

THE BOX (*fig* 36 A and B)

There are several styles and shapes of boxes that can be made up into useful and attractive gifts; in *figure* 36 two different boxes are described – the hinged box and the box with a lid (B).

Both these boxes are made up from separate pieces of card covered with linen and lined with coloured silk; the cut-out design worked on the lids also has a coloured silk background to match the lining of the box.

The joins of the separate pieces of the boxes are embellished by bullion knots; these also serve to hinge the lid of box A. The lid of this box is a fraction larger than the base. A layer of thin wadding placed between the card and the cover of the lid enhances the finished appearance of the box; the inside may also be padded if desired, fastened through with tiny knots to give the inside of the box a quilted appearance. Each separate part of the box must first be cut out in stiff card. Remember to allow sufficient extra material for turning over the raw edges of the linen and the lining.

Great care needs to be taken in stitching the separate pieces of the box together; the stitches should be as invisible as possible, yet it is also very important that each join be firm and erect.

For the box with the fitted lid, the box should be made up first and then the lid made a little bit larger to fit over the edges of the box snugly.

Several suitable designs for ornamenting the lids of both types of box may be found in Chapter VI; the cut-out pattern together with both the padded roll and the open-hem may be worked on the lid, or alternatively the open-hem may decorate the sides of the box.

CHAPTER IX

Layout of Table Linen

TABLE linen has always been chosen, embroidered and treasured with special care and pride by the mistress of the household, not only for its own beauty, but also because it adds charm and distinction to her table when she is entertaining.

Consequently, it is not surprising to find that ever since linen was first ornamented all suitable embroideries have been used to decorate the many items included under this heading. Embroideries such as drawn-work, white work, and cut-work are most effective when worked on table linen in natural linen thread; the shade of the material and thread may match or contrast. However, the wide choice of tableware available today in both traditional and contemporary designs generally calls for the simplicity of self-coloured linen embroidery as a background.

It is essential for table linen not to show signs of wear after it has been laundered a few times. Cut-work has the advantage of being very durable because all the raw edges of the linen have to be well secured into the padded roll before the lace fillings are added.

Cut-work embroidered on table linen shows off the craft to its very best advantage (PLATES 18, 19 and 20). Once the technique has been mastered and the forms and stitches of the simpler patterns learned and practised, the embroideress can proceed to this more interesting and productive field.

Fine hand-woven Italian linen makes up well into tablecloths, sets of table mats, table napkins or cocktail mats, to give some examples. Alternatively, a more hard-wearing quality linen (about 32 threads to the inch) is more suitable for place mats, tray cloths and sideboard runners.

The layout patterns given in this chapter are designed for one yard of either the fine or the coarser linen.

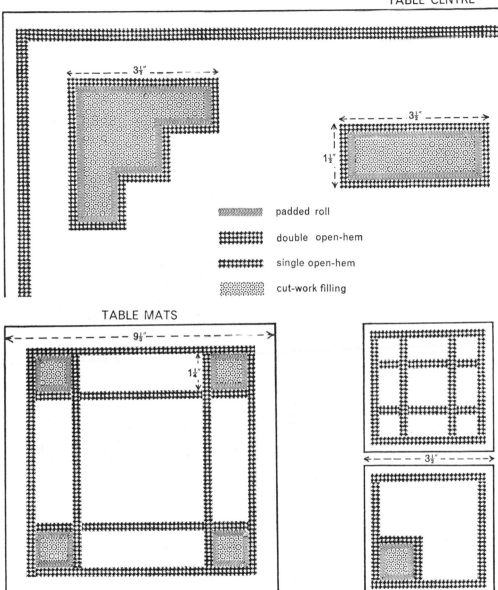

padded roll

double open-hem

single open-hem

cut-work filling

TABLE MATS

Figure 37 is a suggestion for a *table centre* with matching *table mats*. This gives ample scope for various types of fillings using corners, squares and insertion designs.

81

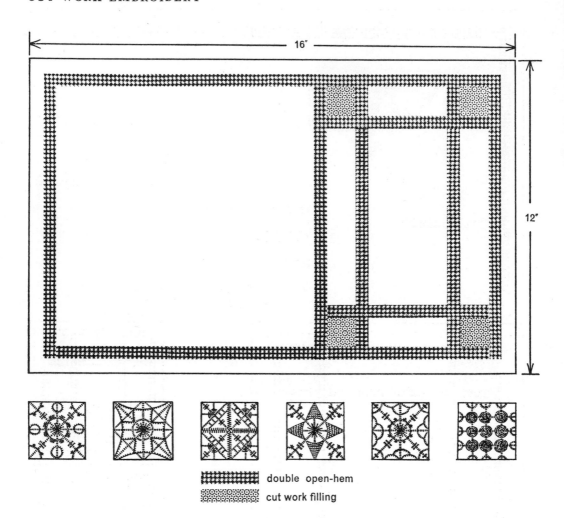

double open-hem

cut work filling

Figure 38 shows a *place mat* made from a piece of linen 18 by 14 inches (thus six mats can be made out of one yard of wider-width material). It has an open-hem framework, and one of the small inset designs may be worked in the corners. The edge of the mat may be ornamented with bullion knots.

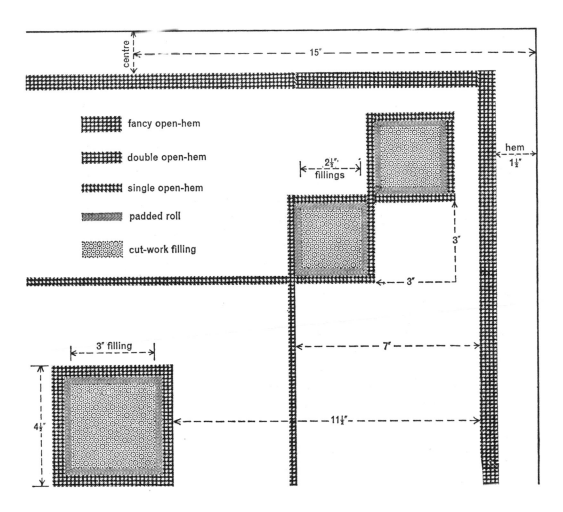

Figure 39 gives the layout for a corner of a square *tablecloth*. Allowance is made for a generous hem, immediately inside which is a framework of fancy open-hem. Draw out the threads as for a double open-hem; then draw another single thread four threads away on either side (see Sampler 1, PLATE 21). The small squares are filled with cut-work, and they are all joined and surrounded by a single open-hem. The larger centre square has a 3-inch filling and is worked inside a double open-hem.

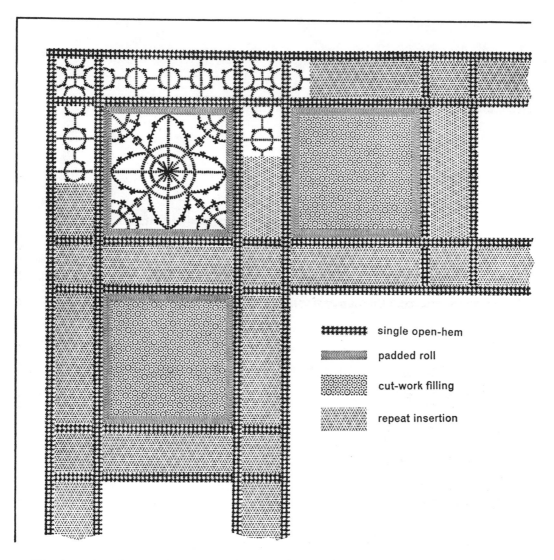

single open-hem

padded roll

cut-work filling

repeat insertion

Figure 40 is a layout for a *trolley cloth* with matching *table napkins*. The cloth has three squares in each corner, which could be filled with different designs, or with repeats of the one design. Work a matching design in one corner of the table napkins. A simple repeat insertion makes an attractive border inside the single open-hem framework, as illustrated above.

CHAPTER X

Neatenings and Finishings

NYTHING creative and hand-made calls for great patience and time; however, time to the true craftsman does not exist, and no detail is too much trouble. Detail of neatening and finishing any piece of work is of the very greatest importance – as much to be proud of as the ornamentation itself. Every piece of embroidery has had the end product in view from the start. The neatening and finishing of the work should also be carefully thought out from the beginning, because the hems, fastenings and joins must be in keeping with the design, material and use for which the finished work is intended.

Hems today tend to be narrower than those of traditional work. This fashion may be followed to advantage, especially when working delicate table linen; but a table-cloth made of a coarser linen looks more attractive with a hem not less than an inch wide.

By tradition corners in cut-work are square, not mitred. The surplus bulk can be cut off before the hem is turned down (*fig* 41 A). The fold of the hem is turned down either on to a single drawn thread, if the hem is to be neatened by hem-stitching; or on to the top of the open-hem and subsequently slip-stitched. At the corner the hem is neatened with invisible slip stitches.

If a hem-stitched neatening is chosen, the hem-stitches themselves will catch down the folds of the hem (A); but if the hem is turned down on to an open-hem (which must be worked first), the edge of the hem must be caught down with slip-stitching (B).

As mentioned in the chapter on edgings, it is characteristic of cut-work to have the edges of the hems embellished with bullion knots or loops of buttonhole stitch (*fig* 32).

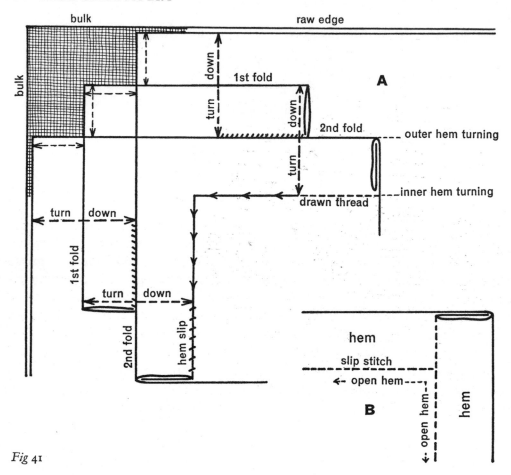

Fig 41

JOINS AND FASTENINGS (*fig* 42)

When small articles need to be lined, padded or even stiffened, bullion knots spaced at half-inch intervals across the edges of the materials (B) make neat and attractive joins. At the corners a single or pair of knots topped by another may alternate with the single knots along the edges.

To hinge a book or box-lid a pair of bullion knots can be used to join the two parts together (A).

The needle-book has pieces of thin felt attached inside the silk lining to carry the assortment of needles. These pieces of felt are first pinked along the edges, and then attached to the silk inside the book by the neat invisible method shown in C.

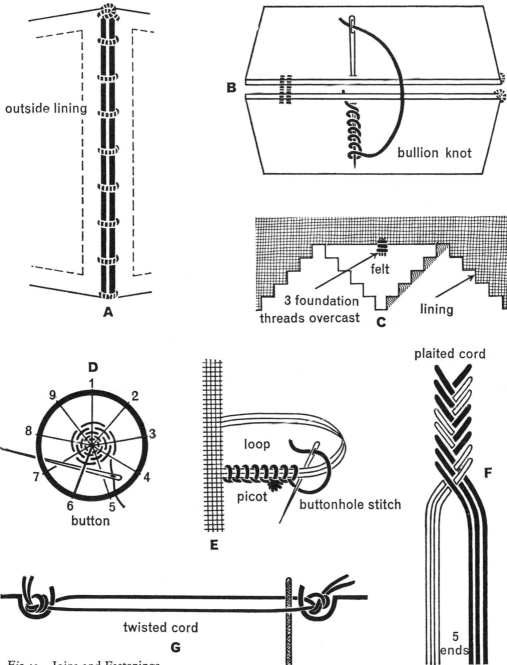

outside lining

A

B bullion knot

3 foundation threads overcast felt lining **C**

D
9 1 2
8 3
7 4
6 5
button

loop
picot buttonhole stitch
E

plaited cord
F
5 ends

twisted cord
G

Fig 42 Joins and Fastenings

Fastenings such as buttons, loops and cords should all be hand-made, to suit the size and style of the finished article. A flat button, woven into a cobweb over a linen-button foundation, is the best type (D). A loop made of a bar of buttonhole stitches worked over three foundation threads presents a neat and adequate fastening (E). (The loop must be measured to fit the size and position of the button.)

Cords of plaited or twisted thread rather thicker than the working thread give a decorative finish to a bag or cushion cover. To make a plaited cord (F) knot together five strands of thread twice the length of the cord required. Pass the outside strand on the right-hand side over two strands, so that it is now in the middle; repeat, using the left-hand strand. Continue in this way until the required length of cord has been plaited. For a twisted cord (G) knot together two lengths of thread at both ends, three times as long as the cord required. Stretch the knotted threads between two hooks. With the threads taut insert a pencil close up to the right-hand knot, and rotate it clockwise until the whole length of thread is firmly twisted. Still keeping the cord taut, place a finger on the centre of the twists, release one end from the hook and fold it over the other end. Remove the pencil and the cord from the second hook, and release the fold, giving it a slight spin; the cord will then twist itself up into its final length.

Index

A CATALOGUE OF
SELECTED DOVER BOOKS
IN ALL FIELDS OF INTEREST

A CATALOGUE OF SELECTED DOVER
BOOKS IN ALL FIELDS OF INTEREST

CONDITIONED REFLEXES, Ivan P. Pavlov. Full translation of most complete statement of Pavlov's work; cerebral damage, conditioned reflex, experiments with dogs, sleep, similar topics of great importance. 430pp. 5⅜ x 8½. 60614-7 Pa. $4.50

NOTES ON NURSING: WHAT IT IS, AND WHAT IT IS NOT, Florence Nightingale. Outspoken writings by founder of modern nursing. When first published (1860) it played an important role in much needed revolution in nursing. Still stimulating. 140pp. 5⅜ x 8½. 22340-X Pa. $3.00

HARTER'S PICTURE ARCHIVE FOR COLLAGE AND ILLUSTRATION, Jim Harter. Over 300 authentic, rare 19th-century engravings selected by noted collagist for artists, designers, decoupeurs, etc. Machines, people, animals, etc., printed one side of page. 25 scene plates for backgrounds. 6 collages by Harter, Satty, Singer, Evans. Introduction. 192pp. 8⅞ x 11¾. 23659-5 Pa. $5.00

MANUAL OF TRADITIONAL WOOD CARVING, edited by Paul N. Hasluck. Possibly the best book in English on the craft of wood carving. Practical instructions, along with 1,146 working drawings and photographic illustrations. Formerly titled *Cassell's Wood Carving*. 576pp. 6½ x 9¼. 23489-4 Pa. $7.95

THE PRINCIPLES AND PRACTICE OF HAND OR SIMPLE TURNING, John Jacob Holtzapffel. Full coverage of basic lathe techniques—history and development, special apparatus, softwood turning, hardwood turning, metal turning. Many projects—billiard ball, works formed within a sphere, egg cups, ash trays, vases, jardiniers, others—included. 1881 edition. 800 illustrations. 592pp. 6⅛ x 9¼. 23365-0 Clothbd. $15.00

THE JOY OF HANDWEAVING, Osma Tod. Only book you need for hand weaving. Fundamentals, threads, weaves, plus numerous projects for small board-loom, two-harness, tapestry, laid-in, four-harness weaving and more. Over 160 illustrations. 2nd revised edition. 352pp. 6½ x 9¼. 23458-4 Pa. $6.00

THE BOOK OF WOOD CARVING, Charles Marshall Sayers. Still finest book for beginning student in wood sculpture. Noted teacher, craftsman discusses fundamentals, technique; gives 34 designs, over 34 projects for panels, bookends, mirrors, etc. "Absolutely first-rate"—E. J. Tangerman. 33 photos. 118pp. 7¾ x 10⅝. 23654-4 Pa. $3.50

AMERICAN ANTIQUE FURNITURE, Edgar G. Miller, Jr. The basic coverage of all American furniture before 1840: chapters per item chronologically cover all types of furniture, with more than 2100 photos. Total of 1106pp. 7⅞ x 10¾.   21599-7, 21600-4 Pa., Two-vol. set $17.90

ILLUSTRATED GUIDE TO SHAKER FURNITURE, Robert Meader. Director, Shaker Museum, Old Chatham, presents up-to-date coverage of all furniture and appurtenances, with much on local styles not available elsewhere. 235 photos. 146pp. 9 x 12.   22819-3 Pa. $6.00

ORIENTAL RUGS, ANTIQUE AND MODERN, Walter A. Hawley. Persia, Turkey, Caucasus, Central Asia, China, other traditions. Best general survey of all aspects: styles and periods, manufacture, uses, symbols and their interpretation, and identification. 96 illustrations, 11 in color. 320pp. 6⅛ x 9¼.   22366-3 Pa. $6.95

CHINESE POTTERY AND PORCELAIN, R. L. Hobson. Detailed descriptions and analyses by former Keeper of the Department of Oriental Antiquities and Ethnography at the British Museum. Covers hundreds of pieces from primitive times to 1915. Still the standard text for most periods. 136 plates, 40 in full color. Total of 750pp. 5⅜ x 8½.
23253-0 Pa. $10.00

THE WARES OF THE MING DYNASTY, R. L. Hobson. Foremost scholar examines and illustrates many varieties of Ming (1368-1644). Famous blue and white, polychrome, lesser-known styles and shapes. 117 illustrations, 9 full color, of outstanding pieces. Total of 263pp. 6⅛ x 9¼. (Available in U.S. only)   23652-8 Pa. $6.00

Prices subject to change without notice.

Available at your book dealer or write for free catalogue to Dept. GI, Dover Publications, Inc., 180 Varick St., N.Y., N.Y. 10014. Dover publishes more than 175 books each year on science, elementary and advanced mathematics, biology, music, art, literary history, social sciences and other areas.